All About Feelings

What Are You Feeling?

Dwayne Booker

SOCIAL AND EMOTIONAL LEARNING FOR THE REAL WORLD™

Rosen Classroom™

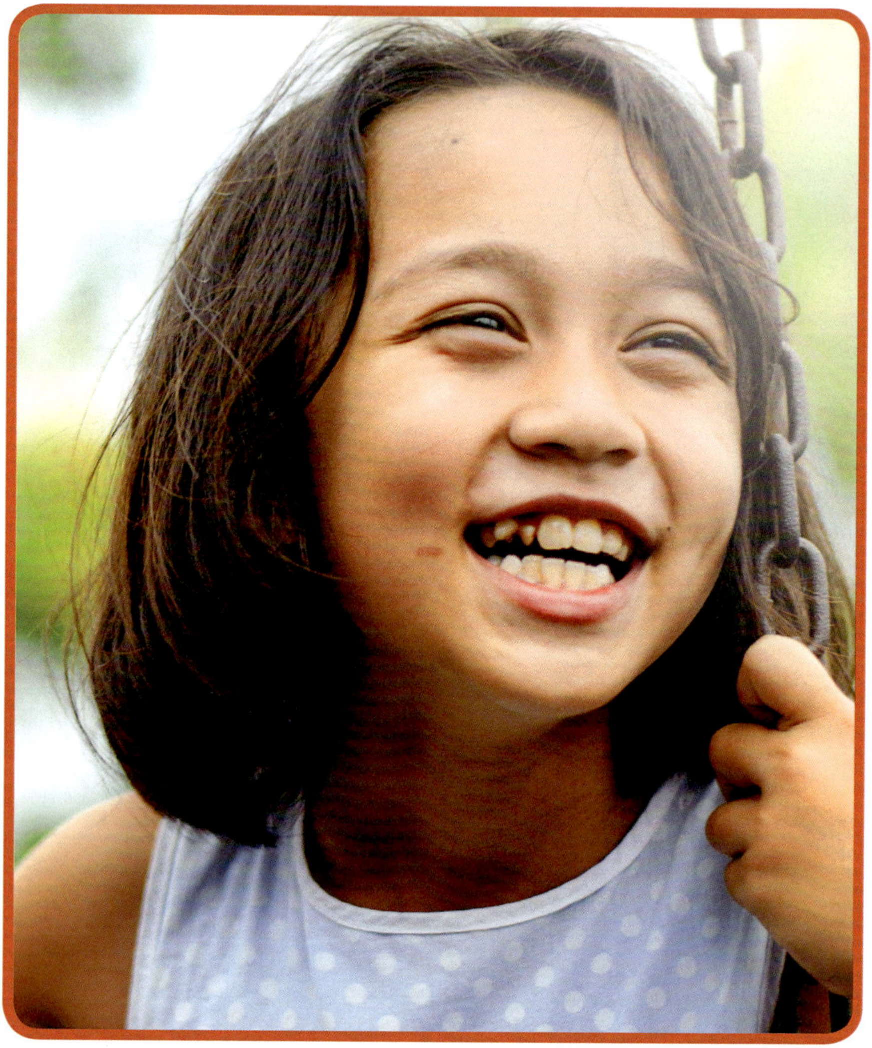

I feel happy.

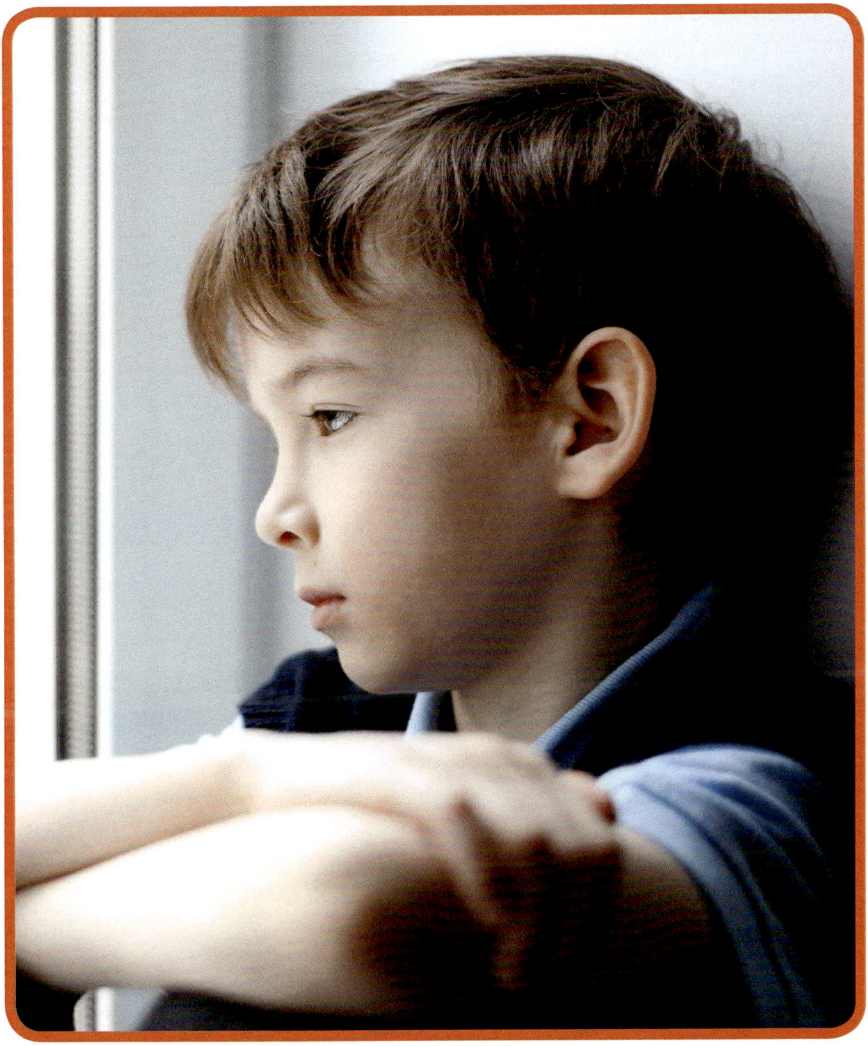

I feel sad.

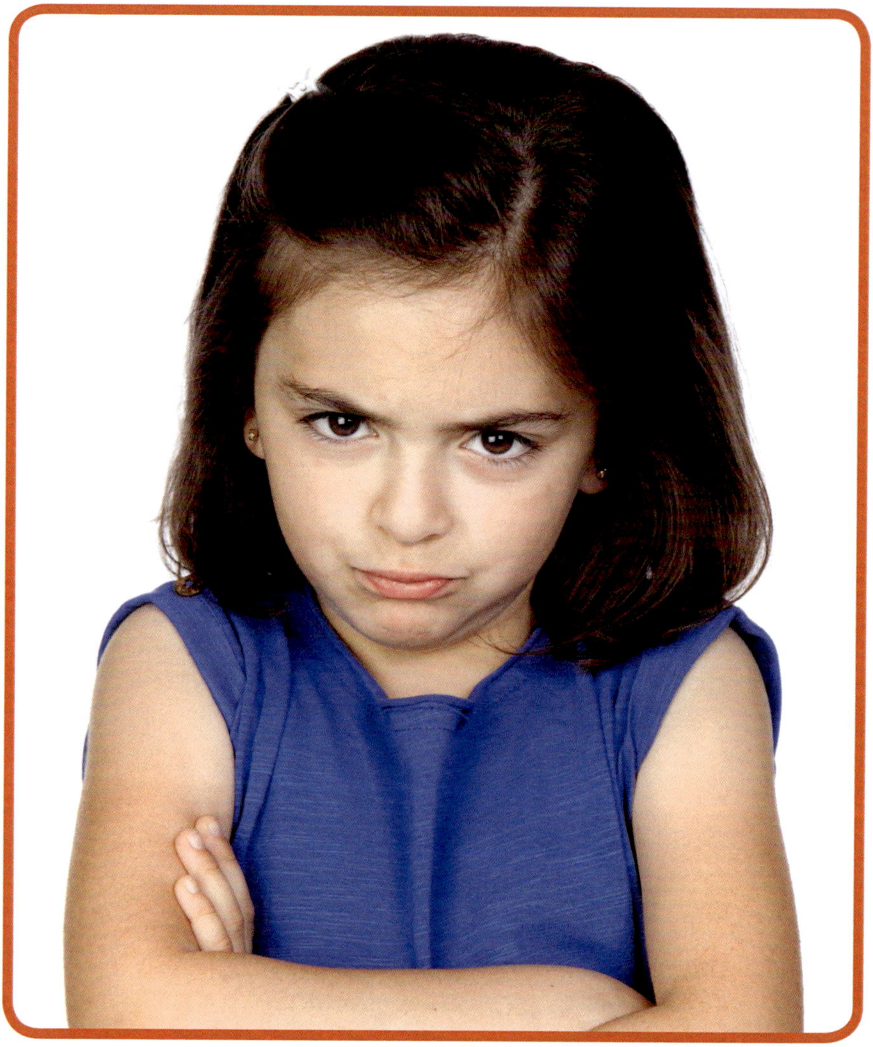

I feel mad.

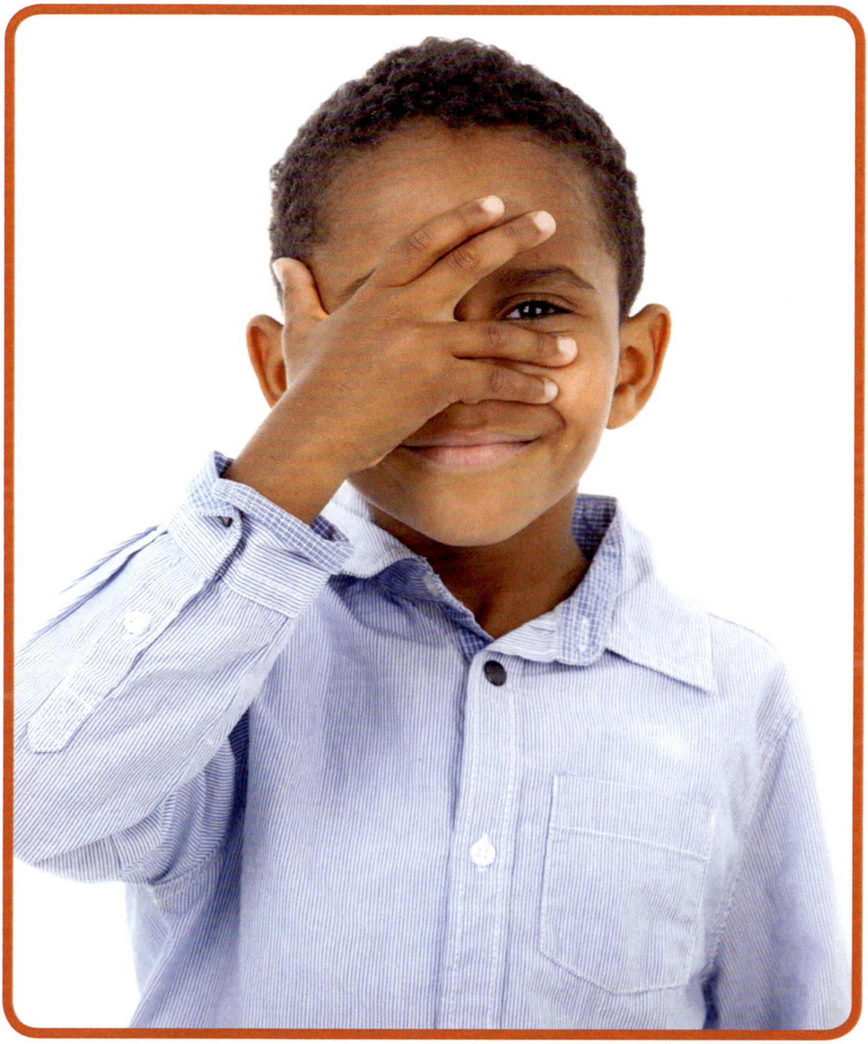

I feel shy.

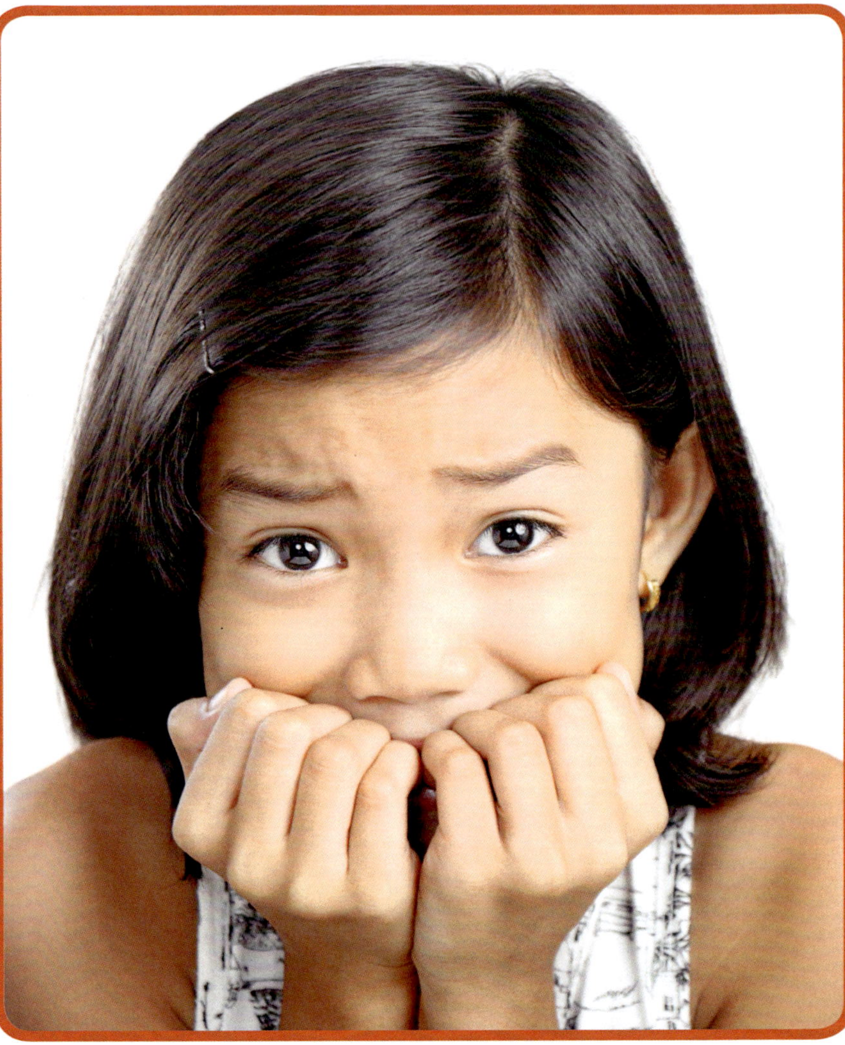

I feel scared.

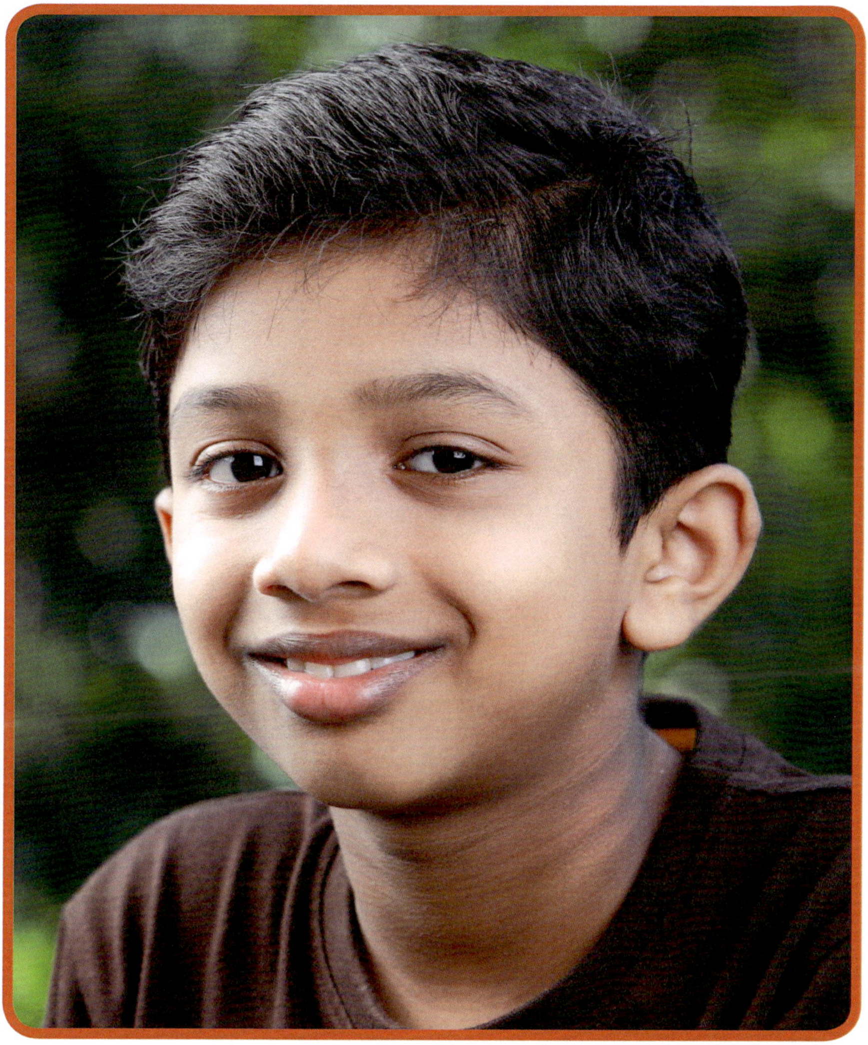

I feel glad.

Words to Know

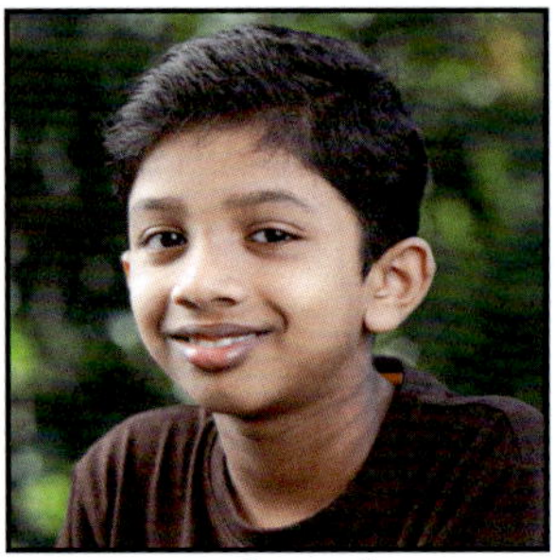
glad

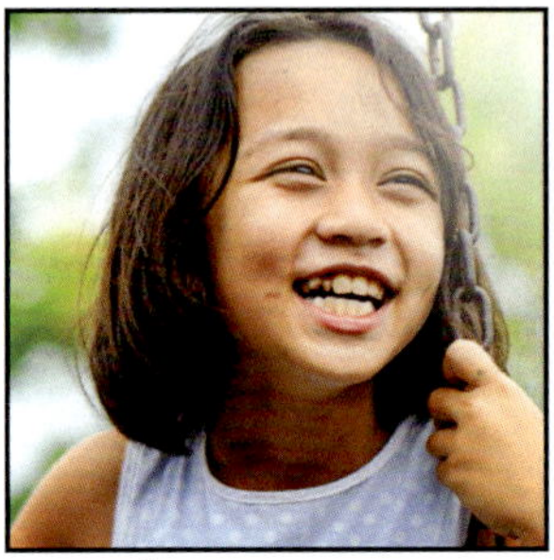
happy

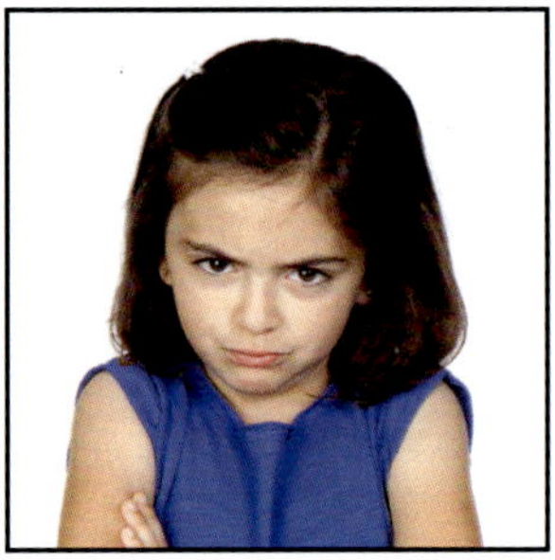
mad

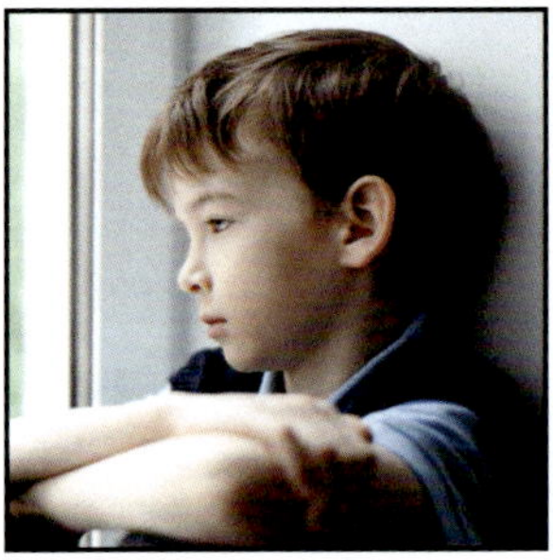
sad

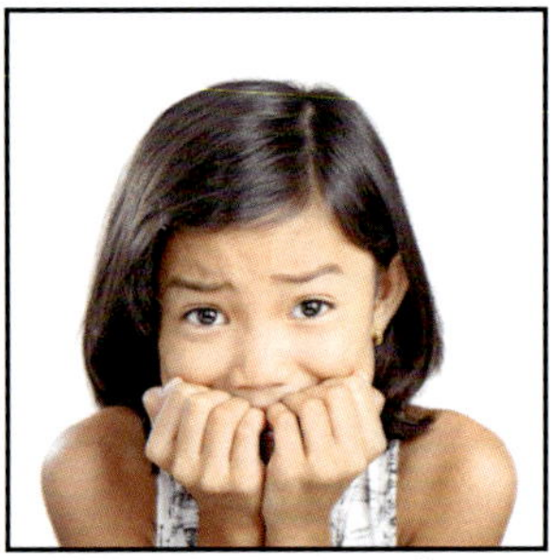
scared

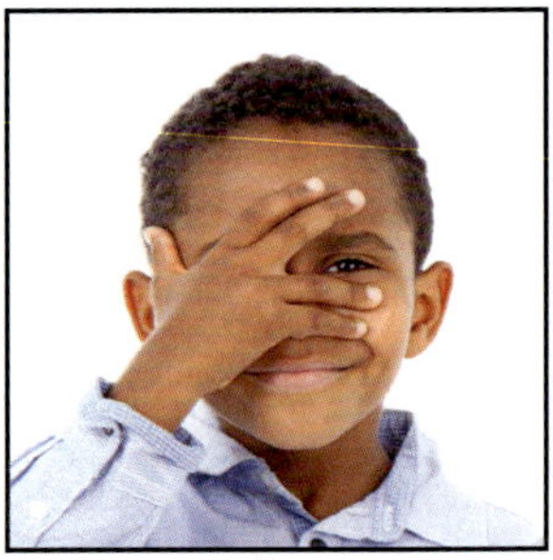
shy